"Endless Ascendance: The Ups and Downs of a Contemporary Tycoon"

Table

"Prepare to embark on a thrilling journey through the world of ambition, wealth, and the intoxicating allure of limitless success. In "Endless Ascendance: The Ups and Downs of a Contemporary Tycoon",' we delve deep into the captivating story of a business magnate whose ascent to the pinnacle of success was matched only by the dizzying descent into the shadows of his own ambition. Join us as we unravel the enigma of an empire built on dreams, shattered by hubris, and discover the timeless lessons hidden within this mesmerizing tale of triumph and tragedy.""Step into a realm where ambition knows no bounds and the pursuit of wealth takes center stage. "Endless Ascendance: The Ups and Downs of a Contemporary Tycoon" is an enthralling journey that invites you to explore the captivating story of a visionary entrepreneur. His ascent to the zenith of success was marked by staggering achievements, only to be followed by a heart-wrenching descent into the depths of his own ambition. This compelling narrative will guide you through the maze of an empire constructed on dreams and eventually shattered by hubris. Join us in unraveling the enigma of this modern tycoon, as we uncover the timeless lessons hidden within this mesmerizing tale of triumph and tragedy.

Chapter 1: The birth of a tycoon

Definition of a tycoon

A tycoon is a prominent figure in a particular industry who has amassed substantial wealth and power while building a business empire. Tycoons are often identified in industries that have economic prominence.

The birth of a tycoon

In the world of business and entrepreneurship, stories of tycoons rising from humble beginnings to amass vast fortunes have always fascinated and inspired us. The journey of a tycoon, marked by ambition, risk-taking, and often a fair share of ups and downs, is a narrative that captures the essence of the American Dream. In this tale, we explore the birth of a new tycoon, their meteoric rise, and the subsequent fall that brought their empire crashing down.

The Genesis: A Visionary's Dream

Our story begins with a young and ambitious individual, who, like many before them, had a vision. This visionary saw opportunities where others saw obstacles and was unafraid to dream big. Their story began with a simple idea, a revolutionary concept that would change the landscape of an industry forever.

The Ascent: From Rags to Riches

With unwavering determination and an unshakeable belief in their idea, this budding tycoon embarked on their journey. They started small, facing countless hurdles, and encountered skepticism at every turn. However, the relentless pursuit of their dream led to the birth of a groundbreaking company. With the right combination of innovation, strategy, and sheer grit, this new tycoon's empire began to grow.

The growth was meteoric, and the company quickly became a household name. Investors clamored to be a part of the success story, and the tycoon's name adorned magazine covers and was celebrated worldwide. The rise to financial prosperity was as swift as it was extraordinary.

The Pinnacle: Living the Dream

At the pinnacle of their success, the new tycoon enjoyed a lifestyle that most could only dream of. They owned luxury homes, private jets, and a fleet of exotic cars. Their name was synonymous with innovation and achievement, and their story served as an inspiration to countless aspiring entrepreneurs.

The Fall: Lessons Learned

However, with great success often comes great pressure. In the pursuit of expansion and profitability, the tycoon made several risky moves. These ventures, once thought to be genius, led to financial pitfalls and legal complications. The empire began to crumble, and the fall from grace was as sudden as the rise to glory.

The lessons learned during this tumultuous period were profound. The new tycoon discovered the perils of complacency, the importance of ethical business practices, and the fickle nature of the market. The fall, though painful, served as a harsh but invaluable teacher.

The Aftermath: A Phoenix Rising

After the fall, the new tycoon faced a crossroads. Some chose to fade into obscurity, forever marked by their rise and fall. Others, however, used the experience as a catalyst for personal and professional growth. They rebuilt, this time with a newfound wisdom and a commitment to making a positive impact on the world.

The birth of a new tycoon is a story of perseverance, ambition, and the unpredictable nature of the business world. It teaches us that success and failure are intertwined in the journey of entrepreneurship, and that, ultimately, the lessons learned during the rise and fall can be as valuable as the riches gained along the way. The saga of ""Endless Ascendance" encapsulates the timeless narrative of tycoons, reminding us that the road to success is fraught with challenges, but it's the ability to rise from the ashes that truly defines a business tycoon's legacy.

The Allure of Infinite Wealth

Wealth has always been a captivating concept, driving people to chase their dreams, work tirelessly, and sometimes take great risks. But there's something uniquely tantalizing about the idea of infinite wealth.

The allure of having limitless resources, an endless stream of riches, and the power to fulfill every desire is a dream that has captured the human imagination for centuries. In this exploration, we delve into the concept of infinite wealth and its profound influence on individuals, societies, and the world at large.

The Illusive Nature of Infinite Wealth: Infinite wealth, by its very definition, implies limitless abundance and resources. It suggests a state where one's financial needs and desires are met without end. However, this concept remains elusive, as wealth, in reality, is finite. No individual or entity possesses truly infinite wealth, as the universe itself has constraints..

Endless Possibilities: The allure of infinite wealth lies in the promise of boundless possibilities. With limitless resources at one's disposal, dreams that seem unattainable to most become achievable. Whether it's creating revolutionary technologies, eradicating poverty, or exploring the cosmos, infinite wealth offers the means to turn these visions into reality.

Power and Influence: Infinite wealth brings with it immeasurable power and influence. Those who possess vast riches can shape the course of economies, politics, and entire societies. They can fund social initiatives, support philanthropic causes, and impact the lives of countless people. The allure of wielding such influence is undeniable.

Freedom and Security:Infinite wealth also offers a sense of unparalleled freedom and security. The fear of financial instability vanishes, and individuals can focus on personal growth, self-fulfillment, and the pursuit of their passions without the constraints of financial worries.

The Dark Side of the Dream:While the allure of infinite wealth is captivating, it often conceals a darker side. The relentless pursuit of wealth can lead to ethical dilemmas, exploitation, and the erosion of one's moral compass. The accumulation of vast fortunes can also create disparities in society, with the rich gaining more power at the expense of the less fortunate.

The Quest for Balance:Balancing the allure of infinite wealth with ethical responsibility is a complex challenge. As individuals, societies, and nations strive to achieve prosperity, it's crucial to consider the impact of wealth on a broader scale and to work towards equitable distribution, responsible wealth management, and sustainable growth.

The allure of infinite wealth continues to captivate the human imagination, driving innovation, ambition, and progress. While the concept remains elusive, it remains a powerful motivator for individuals and societies. However, it's essential to recognize the ethical and moral implications of the pursuit of wealth and work towards a world where prosperity is shared more equitably, ensuring that the allure of wealth does not come at the cost of justice and equality.

Setting the stage

Setting the stage for the rise of a tycoon is a captivating journey that combines ambition, perseverance, and a dash of genius. In the annals of business history, there have been countless tales of individuals who started with humble beginnings and soared to the pinnacle of success. This narrative often begins with a vision, a spark of inspiration, and the determination to turn dreams into reality.

The backdrop for the rise of a tycoon is typically one of challenge and adversity. Many tycoons-to-be come from modest backgrounds, facing economic hardships and limited resources. Yet, it's precisely these constraints that often fuel their determination to achieve greatness. From the steel mills of a young Andrew Carnegie to the small software company founded by Bill Gates in a garage, the stories of tycoons are rife with early struggles and relentless work ethic.

As the story unfolds, one can observe the critical role of innovation and risk-taking. Tycoons are known for their ability to identify opportunities and push the boundaries of convention. Whether it's Elon Musk's pursuit of electric cars and space exploration or the disruptive business model introduced by Jeff Bezos through Amazon, these visionaries often challenge the status quo and redefine entire industries.

The rise of a tycoon is not without its fair share of setbacks and failures. However, it's their resilience and ability to learn from these experiences that set them apart. Each obstacle becomes a stepping stone, and every setback an opportunity for growth. This unwavering determination to overcome adversity is a common thread in the stories of tycoons.

In setting the stage for the rise of a tycoon, we also see the importance of strategic partnerships and networking. Building a team of like-minded individuals who share the same vision is instrumental in achieving success. From the partnership of Steve Jobs and Steve Wozniak at Apple to the collaboration of Larry Page and Sergey Brin at Google, these dynamic duos have reshaped industries.

The journey to becoming a tycoon is also characterized by a commitment to giving back. Many successful entrepreneurs turn their wealth and influence towards philanthropy and social causes. This not only solidifies their legacy but also contributes to positive change in society.

setting the stage for the rise of a tycoon is a narrative rich in determination, innovation, resilience, and a willingness to take calculated risks. From humble beginnings to the pinnacle of success, the journey of a tycoon is a testament to the power of vision and unwavering dedication. It serves as an inspiration for aspiring entrepreneurs and a reminder that with passion and perseverance, even the loftiest dreams can be realized

Chapter 2: The visionary begins

Early Life and Influences

The journey of a tycoon, the embodiment of financial success and power, often begins with a humble and unassuming early life. These individuals, who climb the ladder of success to reach the zenith of their respective industries, are often products of their unique backgrounds and the influential factors that shaped their lives. In this article, we will delve into the early life and influences that have contributed to the rise of various tycoons, highlighting how their experiences and circumstances paved the way for their extraordinary success.

1. Family Background and Support:Many tycoons come from families that played a crucial role in their success. Supportive parents or relatives who encouraged their ambitions and provided educational opportunities laid the foundation for their future achievements. Family businesses, too, often serve as training grounds for

budding tycoons, allowing them to learn the ropes from a young age. Prominent figures like Elon Musk and the Walton family of Walmart owe a significant part of their success to familial support and involvement in business ventures.

2. Educational Background:Education is a common stepping stone for tycoons. Exceptional academic achievements and access to prestigious educational institutions can provide the knowledge and networks necessary for their rise to prominence. Notable examples include Warren Buffett, who received his education at Columbia Business School, and Mark Zuckerberg, who attended Harvard University before founding Facebook.

3. Personal Drive and Ambition:Tycoons are often characterized by an unrelenting drive and ambition. Their early years may be marked by a hunger for success, a desire to make a mark on the world, and a willingness to take calculated risks. Entrepreneurs like Steve Jobs and Jeff Bezos exemplify this trait, having pursued their passions with unwavering determination from a young age.

4. Adversity and Resilience:Adversity can also be a powerful influence in the making of a tycoon. Many

successful individuals have faced significant challenges and setbacks in their early lives, which fueled their determination to overcome obstacles and achieve their goals. Oprah Winfrey, who rose from a troubled childhood to become a media mogul, and Howard Schultz, who turned adversity into success by founding Starbucks, are prime examples.

5. Mentorship and Networking:Mentors and influential connections often play a pivotal role in a tycoon's journey. They can provide guidance, advice, and opportunities that propel individuals to greater heights. The mentorship of figures like Bill Gates by Warren Buffett, or the professional networks that figures like Richard Branson have cultivated, has been instrumental in shaping their success.

The early life and influences that contribute to the rise of a tycoon are diverse and multi-faceted. These individuals come from various backgrounds and have experienced different circumstances that have shaped their paths to success. While family support, education, personal drive, adversity, and mentorship are just a few of the influential factors, the common thread that ties these tycoons together is their unwavering determination to overcome obstacles and reach the pinnacle of their industries. Their stories serve as inspiration for aspiring entrepreneurs and demonstrate that the journey to becoming a tycoon can begin in the most unexpected places.

Building the empire

Title: The Rise of a Tycoon: Building an Empire from Scratch

In the world of business and entrepreneurship, there are individuals who rise above the rest, building vast empires from scratch. These visionaries are often referred to as "tycoons." Their stories of success are not just tales of wealth and power; they are journeys of ambition, innovation, and relentless determination. This content delves into the steps and principles behind the rise of a tycoon and the art of building an empire.

1. Vision and Ambition:Every tycoon's journey begins with a grand vision and boundless ambition. They dream big and set audacious goals. Their ability to see opportunities where others see challenges is a defining trait. A vision becomes the driving force, motivating them to take risks and push the boundaries of conventional thinking.

2. Risk-Taking:Building an empire often involves taking calculated risks. Tycoons understand that without risk, there is no reward. They are not afraid to invest significant resources, whether it's time, money, or effort, into their vision. Learning to assess and manage risks is a crucial skill on the path to empire-building.

3. Innovation:Tycoons thrive on innovation. They create or identify disruptive ideas and technologies that can change industries. By staying ahead of the curve and continuously evolving, they ensure their empires remain relevant and competitive.

4. Resilience:Obstacles and setbacks are a part of any entrepreneur's journey. Tycoons possess extraordinary resilience. They do not let failures deter them. Instead, they view setbacks as opportunities to learn and grow. This ability to bounce back is a key factor in their success.

5. Building a Team:No tycoon builds an empire alone. They assemble talented teams that complement their skills and vision. Strong leadership and the ability to inspire and motivate a workforce are critical. Trusting and empowering their team members is essential for sustainable growth.

6. Strategic Partnerships:Tycoons often forge strategic partnerships and alliances to expand their reach and influence. These partnerships can open doors to new markets, resources, and expertise. Successful empire builders are skilled in negotiation and relationship management.

7. Long-Term Focus:While tycoons may seize short-term opportunities, they have a long-term perspective. They understand that building an empire is a marathon, not a sprint. This patience and focus on sustainable growth ensure the empire's longevity.

8. Adaptation and Evolution:Industries change, markets fluctuate, and consumer preferences evolve. Tycoons adapt and evolve with these changes. They are open to new ideas and pivot when necessary to stay ahead of the curve.

9. Philanthropy and Legacy:Many tycoons understand the importance of giving back to society. They establish philanthropic foundations and initiatives to make a positive impact on the world. This not only leaves a lasting legacy but also contributes to the betterment of society.

The rise of a tycoon and the building of an empire is a remarkable journey that encompasses vision, ambition, risk-taking, innovation, resilience, teamwork, partnerships, long-term focus, and adaptation. These individuals serve as inspiration for aspiring entrepreneurs, showing that with the right mindset and determination, anyone can achieve great success and create a lasting legacy. Building an empire is not just about accumulating wealth; it's about leaving a mark on the world that will endure for generations to come.

Chapter 3:The rise of power

- Market Dominance

In the realm of business and commerce, the ascent of a tycoon is often an awe-inspiring spectacle. These individuals possess the extraordinary ability to not only succeed but to dominate their respective markets. Market dominance is the pinnacle of entrepreneurial achievement, and it is achieved through a combination of strategy, innovation, and unwavering determination.

The Birth of a Visionary:

The journey of a tycoon begins with a visionary leader who identifies an opportunity in the market. Whether it's a groundbreaking technology, an untapped consumer need, or a disruptive business model, these individuals have a unique ability to spot what others may overlook. This vision serves as the foundation for their ascent to market dominance.

Innovation as the Cornerstone:

Innovation is the driving force behind the rise of a tycoon. They are unafraid to challenge the status quo, pushing the boundaries of what is possible. This commitment to innovation allows them to create products or services that are not only superior but also revolutionize the industry. Steve Jobs, with the introduction of the iPhone, is a prime example of how innovation can catapult a company to market dominance.

Strategic Mastery:

A tycoon's journey to market dominance is guided by strategic acumen. They understand the market, their competitors, and the evolving needs of consumers. Their strategic thinking is long-term and adaptable, enabling them to navigate through market fluctuations and disruptions effectively.

Relentless Pursuit of Excellence:

The pursuit of excellence is a hallmark of a tycoon. They set high standards for their products and services, demanding nothing less than perfection. This unwavering commitment to quality and customer satisfaction fosters loyalty and trust, which are essential for maintaining market dominance.

Building a Strong Team:

No tycoon rises to the top alone. They surround themselves with a talented and dedicated team. These individuals share the tycoon's vision and are instrumental in executing the strategy. A strong team enables the tycoon to scale their operations and maintain their market dominance.

Adaptability and Resilience:

The path to market dominance is rarely a smooth one. Tycoons face challenges, setbacks, and fierce competition. What sets them apart is their resilience and ability to adapt. They learn from failures and continue to evolve, ensuring they remain at the forefront of their industry.

The Ripple Effect:

The rise of a tycoon and their subsequent market dominance often has a profound impact. It can lead to industry-wide transformations, inspiring others to innovate and compete at a higher level. Additionally, it can create economic opportunities and jobs, benefiting not only the tycoon but also the broader community.

the rise of a tycoon to market dominance is a remarkable journey fueled by vision, innovation, strategy, and a relentless pursuit of excellence. Their stories serve as a testament to the power of entrepreneurial spirit and the potential for individuals to leave an indelible mark on the business world. It is a testament to what is possible when extraordinary individuals embark on a journey to change the world.

Title: Unconventional Strategies for the Rise of a New Tycoon

In the ever-evolving landscape of business and entrepreneurship, the path to becoming a new tycoon is no longer limited to traditional methods. In this era of innovation and disruption, unconventional strategies are increasingly playing a crucial role in catapulting individuals to the status of industry leaders. Here are some unique and unconventional strategies that can pave the way for the rise of a new tycoon:

1.Niche Saturation: Instead of trying to conquer broad markets, some new tycoons focus on niche markets that are often overlooked. By deeply understanding the needs and desires of a small, passionate audience, they can dominate that niche and become the go-to authority within it. This strategy allows for exponential growth within a specific segment.

2. Leverage the Power of the Internet:The internet has democratized entrepreneurship. New tycoons often harness the global reach of the internet to create and promote their products or services. From influencer marketing to online courses and e-commerce, the digital realm provides a vast playground for those willing to explore it.

3. Reverse Engineering Success:Instead of trying to reinvent the wheel, some new tycoons reverse engineer the success of existing businesses. They identify what makes other companies successful and adapt those strategies to their own ventures. This

approach can provide a shortcut to success by learning from the experiences of others.

4. Crowdsourced Capital: Crowdfunding platforms have enabled many aspiring tycoons to raise capital for their projects. By presenting their ideas to the public and offering incentives or equity, they can secure funding without the need for traditional investors. This approach allows for creative and innovative ideas to take flight.

5. Radical Transparency: Some new tycoons adopt a radically transparent approach to their businesses. They share everything from financials to decision-making processes with their customers and stakeholders. This level of openness builds trust and loyalty, often resulting in a passionate following and rapid growth.

6. Gowth Hacking Growth hacking is a marketing strategy that leverages creative and unconventional tactics to accelerate business growth. New tycoons often use these strategies to quickly gain a competitive advantage, whether through social media stunts, guerrilla marketing, or viral content.

7. Microbranding: Building a personal brand around an individual's expertise or personality can be a highly effective strategy. By becoming a recognized authority

in a specific field or industry, new tycoons can attract opportunities, partnerships, and customers who are drawn to their unique personal brand.

8. Sustainable and Social Impact:Businesses with a strong focus on sustainability and social impact are gaining traction. New tycoons who prioritize these values often find that they can attract a passionate customer base, partnerships, and investors who align with their mission.

9. Gamification: Incorporating game-like elements into products and services can enhance user engagement and create a loyal customer base. New tycoons who adopt gamification in their offerings can make the user experience more enjoyable and addictive.

10.   Decentralization:Embracing   decentralized technologies like blockchain and decentralized finance (DeFi) can provide opportunities for new tycoons. These technologies offer innovative ways to disrupt traditional industries and create new revenue streams.

In conclusion, the path to becoming a new tycoon is no longer bound by conventional norms. Unconventional strategies, along with creativity and innovation, can propel individuals to success in ways that were previously unimaginable. By embracing these unique approaches, aspiring entrepreneurs can increase their chances of making a significant impact in the business world..

A tycoon philosophy

The concept of a "tycoon" conjures images of individuals who have reached the zenith of wealth and influence in their respective industries. Tycoons are not merely rich; they are visionaries, risk-takers, and trailblazers. What underlies the rise of a tycoon is not just financial acumen but also a unique philosophy that guides their journey. In this article, we explore the tycoon philosophy and the principles that pave the way for aspiring tycoons to reach the pinnacle of success.

1. Vision and Ambition:Tycoons start with a grand vision and an unquenchable ambition. They see opportunities where others see obstacles. The tycoon philosophy revolves around the idea that thinking big is the first step to achieving something extraordinary. Elon Musk's vision of colonizing Mars and Jeff Bezos' dream of commercial space travel are testament to this philosophy.

2. Innovation and Risk-Taking:Tycoons are not afraid to disrupt the status quo. They embrace innovation and are willing to take calculated risks. They understand that without risk, there can be no substantial rewards. The philosophy here is to be fearless in the face of uncertainty, like Mark Zuckerberg's bold move to transform Facebook into a global social media giant.

3. Continuous Learning:Learning is a fundamental aspect of the tycoon philosophy. Tycoons are voracious readers and lifelong learners. They recognize that the business landscape is constantly evolving, and to stay at the top, one must adapt and acquire new knowledge. Warren Buffett, the Oracle of Omaha, is an excellent example of a tycoon who emphasizes continuous learning.

4. Persistence and Resilience:The road to tycoon status is often paved with setbacks and failures. The tycoon philosophy teaches individuals to be persistent and resilient. Failure is not a roadblock but a stepping stone to success. Oprah Winfrey, who rose from poverty and adversity to become a media mogul, exemplifies the unwavering determination of a tycoon.

5. Networking and Relationships:Building and nurturing relationships is a crucial part of the tycoon philosophy.

Tycoons understand the value of connections in business and life. They leverage their networks for opportunities and support. Richard Branson, known for his Virgin Group empire, is a master networker who emphasizes the importance of building strong relationships.

6. Social Responsibility:The modern tycoon philosophy includes a sense of social responsibility. Many tycoons engage in philanthropy and contribute to causes that are important to them. Bill Gates, through the Gates Foundation, has dedicated a significant portion of his wealth to addressing global issues like healthcare and education.

7. Adapting to Change:Adaptability is key in the tycoon philosophy. Industries and markets change rapidly, and tycoons must be agile in response to these changes. The ability to pivot and adapt to new circumstances is a hallmark of successful tycoons like Steve Jobs, who reinvented Apple multiple times.

The rise of a tycoon is not solely about accumulating wealth; it's a journey that encompasses vision, ambition, innovation, resilience, and a commitment to lifelong learning. The tycoon philosophy is a guiding set of principles that lead individuals toward becoming influential figures in their respective fields. While not everyone can reach the pinnacle of tycoon status, adopting some of these philosophies can lead to personal and professional growth, and perhaps even the realization of extraordinary dreams.

Chapters 4:Infinite Wealth and Opulence

Excesses and Extravagance

The journey from rags to riches is often a compelling tale of ambition, hard work, and determination. Tycoons, those who amass substantial wealth and influence, frequently find themselves at a crossroads when it comes to excess and extravagance. While their success enables them to indulge in opulent lifestyles, it's essential to examine the repercussions of such choices.

The Tycoon's Dilemma:

1. Financial Prosperity:

Tycoons often accumulate immense wealth through their business acumen and innovation. The allure of financial success can lead to the desire for excessive spending, including luxury homes, yachts, private jets, and extravagant parties.

2. Social Status and Recognition:

The public often equates wealth with prestige. Tycoons may feel pressured to display their success through high-profile philanthropy, conspicuous consumption, and a constant presence in the media.

3. **Responsibility to Society

Tycoons have the means to make a significant impact on society. However, the pursuit of excess may overshadow their potential for philanthropy and contributions to pressing social and environmental issues.

4. **Work-Life Balance**:

The path to tycoon status often involves relentless dedication to one's business. Balancing personal life and leisure with the demands of entrepreneurship can be challenging, leading to stress and burnout.

5.*Public Scrutiny:

The actions of tycoons are scrutinized by the public, and the line between genuine philanthropy and self-promotion can be thin. This public attention can lead to ethical dilemmas.

Striking a Balance:
To mitigate the risks associated with excess and extravagance, tycoons can consider the following strategies:

1. Financial Prudence: Maintain a disciplined approach to personal finances, with careful budgeting and financial planning.
2. Philanthropic Endeavors: Channel wealth and resources toward meaningful philanthropic causes to make a positive impact on society.
3. Sustainability: Invest in environmentally responsible practices and support sustainable business initiatives.
4. Work-Life Harmony:Prioritize personal well-being and family life to prevent burnout.
5. Transparent Philanthropy:Engage in philanthropy with transparency and sincerity to avoid public skepticism.

The rise of a tycoon presents a unique set of challenges and opportunities when it comes to navigating the temptations of excess and extravagance. Achieving a balance between personal indulgence and responsible stewardship of wealth is not only essential for the tycoon's well-being but also for the betterment of society. By making mindful choices and leveraging their success for the greater good, tycoons can transform their wealth into a positive force for change, leaving a lasting legacy beyond material opulence.

. luxurious lifestyle

In a world where success often equates to wealth, the concept of a luxurious lifestyle is a tantalizing dream for many. It's a vision of opulence, comfort, and indulgence that has become synonymous with the rise of a tycoon. To understand this connection, we must delve into the journey of a tycoon and how it leads to a life of luxury.

The Path to Tycoon Status:

Tycoons, by definition, are individuals who have reached the pinnacle of their respective industries, amassing significant wealth and influence. Their journey is marked by relentless ambition, unparalleled dedication, and a remarkable ability to turn vision into reality. These individuals often possess a unique combination of innovation, entrepreneurship, and strategic thinking that propels them to the top.

The Relationship with Luxury:

As tycoons climb the ladder of success, they accumulate vast fortunes through their business ventures, investments, or innovations. This newfound wealth opens the door to a luxurious lifestyle that may include:

1. Exquisite Residences: Tycoons often reside in sprawling mansions, penthouses in the world's most coveted locations, or even private islands. These properties are equipped with the latest technology, stunning architecture, and awe-inspiring views.

2. Extravagant Vehicles: Luxury cars, private jets, and yachts are common indulgences for tycoons. These high-end vehicles not only provide convenience but also serve as symbols of their success.

3. Fine Dining and Travel: Dining at Michelin-starred restaurants and traveling in style on private jets are just a few of the ways tycoons savor the finer things in life. Their journeys are marked by exclusivity and extravagance.

4. Collectibles and Art: Many tycoons are avid collectors of rare art, vintage wine, or unique memorabilia. These collections not only hold personal value but often appreciate in worth over time.

5. Philanthropy and Social Engagement: While the luxury lifestyle is appealing, many tycoons also channel their wealth into philanthropic endeavors, contributing to causes they are passionate about and leaving a lasting legacy.

The Luxury Paradox:

The rise of a tycoon and the subsequent embrace of a luxurious lifestyle can be a double-edged sword. On one hand, it represents the rewards of hard work, innovation, and determination. On the other hand, it can lead to criticism and scrutiny regarding income inequality and conspicuous consumption. Tycoons often find themselves balancing their desire for opulence with their responsibility to society., the link between a luxurious lifestyle and the rise of a tycoon is undeniable. The pursuit of success often leads these individuals to unprecedented wealth, enabling them to enjoy the finest things in life. However, the path to tycoon status is marked by challenges, sacrifices, and a relentless pursuit of excellence. It's a journey that showcases the intricate relationship between ambition, achievement, and the allure of luxury.

Chapter 5: A tycoon downfall

The Crash and Its Impact

The Crash and Its Impact on a Tycoon's Downfall"

The Crash, often used to refer to economic downturns or stock market collapses, can have far-reaching consequences, especially for high-profile tycoons and magnates. These individuals, who have often amassed immense wealth and power, are not immune to the effects of market volatility and financial crises. In this article, we'll explore how "The Crash" can lead to a tycoon's downfall and the profound impact it has on their fortunes and legacies.

The Tycoon's Ascent

Before delving into the consequences of "The Crash," it's essential to understand the typical trajectory of a tycoon's rise. These individuals often accumulate wealth through successful business ventures, strategic investments, or entrepreneurial brilliance. Over time, they amass vast empires, command significant influence in various industries, and even shape economies with their actions.

The Crash: A Harsh Reality Check

When "The Crash" occurs, it signifies a sudden and severe economic downturn, characterized by a sharp decline in stock prices, economic growth, and business profitability. Tycoons, with their extensive financial interests, are highly exposed to these fluctuations. Whether it's a stock market crash, a housing bubble burst, or a recession, the impact can be devastating.

Wealth Erosion

The first and most direct consequence of "The Crash" on a tycoon is the erosion of wealth. Their fortunes, often tied to investments, company valuations, and stock portfolios, can plummet rapidly. Billion-dollar empires can lose significant value within days or even hours. This can lead to a substantial reduction in net worth, affecting the tycoon's ability to finance projects, maintain their luxurious lifestyle, or retain their status on global rich lists.

Strained Business Holdings

Tycoons typically hold diverse portfolios of businesses and investments. When a financial crisis strikes, it can severely strain these holdings. Companies may face declining revenues, reduced consumer spending, and difficulties in accessing credit. This can result in layoffs, bankruptcies, and even the collapse of entire business empires. Tycoons must grapple with the challenge of saving their business interests or, in some cases, letting them go.

Debt and Leverage

High-profile tycoons often utilize leverage to magnify their investments. They borrow large sums of money to finance ventures, believing that their success will allow them to repay the debts with ease. However, during "The Crash," the value of their assets can plummet, leaving them with massive debts and little collateral. Managing this debt in the midst of a financial crisis can be extremely challenging and can lead to a tycoon's downfall.

Reputation and Legacy

Beyond the financial repercussions, a tycoon's reputation and legacy can also be severely impacted. Once celebrated as visionaries and economic powerhouses, they may face public scrutiny, criticism, and legal challenges if their actions are perceived as contributing to the financial crisis. This tarnished reputation can have long-lasting consequences, affecting their social standing and philanthropic endeavors.

The Road to Recovery

While "The Crash" can lead to a tycoon's downfall, it's important to note that not all tycoons are permanently dethroned. Some may recover from financial setbacks through resilience, adaptability, and strategic decision-making. Others may choose to reinvent themselves or shift their focus toward philanthropy and social responsibility.

"The Crash" and its impact on a tycoon's downfall serves as a stark reminder of the vulnerability of even the most powerful and wealthy individuals to the unpredictability of financial markets. The consequences can be profound, affecting wealth, businesses, reputation, and legacy. It underscores the importance of diversification, risk management, and responsible financial practices in the world of high-stakes entrepreneurship and investment.

Chapter6:legacy and controversy

The Tycoon's Influence

In the world of business and industry, tycoons are often seen as powerful figures who shape the course of economies and societies. Their influence can be immense, both in the business world and in the wider political and social spheres. However, this influence can sometimes lead to the eventual fall of these titans of industry, as their power and ambition come under scrutiny.

The Rise of a Tycoon:

Tycoons typically begin their journeys as visionary entrepreneurs with innovative ideas and unrelenting determination. They build their empires from the ground up, taking risks and making bold decisions that set them apart from the competition. Their influence starts to grow as they accumulate wealth, expand their businesses, and often diversify into various industries. The tycoon's reach extends into politics, philanthropy, and even popular culture. Their charisma and leadership become the driving forces behind their ever-expanding influence.

The Zenith of Power:

At the height of their success, tycoons wield incredible power, often making decisions that impact the lives of millions. Their influence extends to shaping public policies, influencing government officials, and even altering the course of entire industries. They become household names, admired for their achievements and feared for their control over markets and resources. This zenith of power, however, can be a double-edged sword.

The Fall of a Tycoon:

The fall of a tycoon can be swift and dramatic, driven by a variety of factors. These may include legal issues, ethical controversies, financial mismanagement, or changing market dynamics. As their influence grows, they sometimes overstep boundaries or become entangled in scandals that tarnish their reputations. This can lead to investigations, legal battles, and public outrage.

Moreover, as industries evolve, new players emerge, and disruptive technologies reshape markets, the once-dominant tycoon may find it challenging to adapt. Failure to embrace change and evolve can accelerate their decline. Economic downturns or financial crises can also expose vulnerabilities in their vast empires.

The Aftermath:

The fall of a tycoon often has far-reaching consequences. It can lead to the unraveling of their business empire, affecting employees, shareholders, and the broader economy. Legal proceedings, fines, and even imprisonment can be the price they pay for their actions. Their influence, once revered, is replaced by a sense of caution and skepticism.

the rise and fall of a tycoon is a fascinating and cautionary tale of power, ambition, and the consequences of unchecked influence. While tycoons can shape industries and societies, their downfall serves as a reminder that no one is above the law, and that with great power comes great responsibility. The story of the tycoon's influence is a timeless narrative of triumph and tragedy, reminding us of the delicate balance between success and hubris in the world of business and beyond.

- Ongoing Legal Battles

Title: Ongoing Legal Battles and the Fall of a Tycoon

In the high-stakes world of business and finance, the rise and fall of tycoons often make for compelling narratives. Over the years, we have witnessed numerous prominent figures who have amassed great wealth and power, only to see their empires crumble as a result of legal battles. These ongoing legal battles shed light on the complexities of financial misconduct, corporate malfeasance, and the accountability of even the most influential individuals.

One such example is the recent downfall of a once-mighty tycoon whose empire was built on a foundation of questionable business practices. As allegations of financial impropriety and corporate wrongdoing came to the forefront, it became evident that the legal system would play a pivotal role in unraveling the intricate web of deception that had been woven over years.

The legal battles surrounding the fall of this tycoon have been multi-faceted, ranging from criminal charges to civil lawsuits. Some of the key aspects of this ongoing legal saga include:

1. Criminal Investigations: Law enforcement agencies have initiated investigations into allegations of fraud, money laundering, and other criminal activities. These investigations have revealed a pattern of financial misconduct that has had far-reaching consequences.

2. Securities Fraud: The tycoon and their associates are facing allegations of manipulating stock prices, misrepresenting financial information, and engaging in insider trading. These actions have led to significant losses for investors and shareholders.

3. Regulatory Scrutiny: Regulatory bodies have also stepped in to examine the company's operations,

seeking to hold the tycoon accountable for any violations of securities and corporate governance laws. This regulatory scrutiny has highlighted the need for stronger oversight in the business world.

4. Civil Litigation: A wave of civil lawsuits has been filed against the tycoon and their company by disgruntled investors, creditors, and business partners who claim to have suffered financial harm as a result of the tycoon's actions.

5. Asset Forfeiture: Authorities are pursuing legal avenues to seize and liquidate the tycoon's assets to compensate those who have been harmed by their actions. The tycoon's lavish lifestyle, once a symbol of opulence, is now under scrutiny as these legal battles progress.

The ongoing legal battles in the wake of the tycoon's fall underscore the importance of accountability and the role of the legal system in addressing financial misconduct. They also serve as a reminder that even the most powerful individuals and corporations are not above the law.

As these legal battles continue to unfold, the public eagerly awaits the outcomes and the potential precedents they may set. The fall of a tycoon, while a cautionary tale, also provides an opportunity for the legal system to demonstrate its commitment to justice and fairness, regardless of one's position or wealth.

Chapter 7

<u>Rebuilding or retiring</u>

Title: Rebuilding or Retiring: The Fall of a Tycoon

In the world of business, the rise and fall of tycoons is a common narrative. While the ascent to the summit of success is often celebrated, the fall from grace can be equally, if not more, compelling. This article delves into the complexities of rebuilding or retiring when a business tycoon experiences a dramatic downfall.

The Tycoon's Downfall

The fall of a business tycoon is often accompanied by a myriad of challenges, including financial losses, tarnished reputations, and legal battles. It can be triggered by various factors such as economic downturns, corporate scandals, or personal mismanagement. When this fall happens, the tycoon faces a pivotal crossroads: should they attempt to rebuild their empire or gracefully retire from the business world?

Rebuilding: A Herculean Task

For many fallen tycoons, the idea of rebuilding their empire holds great allure. They are driven by a desire to rectify past mistakes and regain their lost glory. Rebuilding often involves significant personal sacrifices, the restructuring of their businesses, and a relentless commitment to redemption. It may require seeking new investors, forming strategic partnerships, and meticulously managing their assets.

Rebuilding also demands a deep reflection on what went wrong. Tycoons must learn from their failures and implement changes to prevent a repeat of past mistakes. This process can be a long and arduous journey, but for those with unwavering determination, it is possible.

Retiring with Dignity

On the other hand, some tycoons choose to gracefully retire from the business world after their fall. Retiring can mean closing down their businesses, liquidating assets, and settling outstanding debts. It's an acknowledgment that the path of rebuilding is too treacherous or that the desire to reclaim past glory has waned.

Retiring with dignity allows tycoons to focus on personal growth, philanthropic endeavors, or even mentoring the next generation of entrepreneurs. It can be an opportunity to make amends for past wrongs and give back to society.

The Path Less Traveled

The decision to rebuild or retire is a deeply personal one, and it often depends on a variety of factors, including the tycoon's financial resources, their emotional resilience, and their support network. While many opt for the path of rebuilding, choosing retirement can be equally courageous. It's a testament to the belief that there's more to life than the pursuit of wealth and power.

The fall of a business tycoon can be a humbling and transformative experience. It offers an opportunity for introspection, growth, and the choice to rebuild or retire. Both paths have their challenges and rewards, but what truly matters is the lesson learned and the legacy left behind. Whether a tycoon decides to rebuild their empire or retire with dignity, the fall is a reminder that even the mightiest can stumble, and it's how they rise or gracefully exit that defines their character.

A new chapter

In the wake of adversity, a once-thriving tycoon embarks on a journey of resilience and reinvention. This new chapter in their life is a story of redemption, determination, and the unyielding spirit of entrepreneurship.

The fall of the tycoon, previously at the peak of their success, seemed like the end of an era. Economic downturns, personal setbacks, and unexpected challenges had brought them to their knees. However, it was in this crucible of despair that they found the spark to rise once again.

The first step in their revival was a deep reflection on the lessons learned from their past successes and failures. They recognized that the true essence of entrepreneurship lay not just in accumulating wealth, but in the ability to adapt, innovate, and persevere.

With renewed vigor, the tycoon set out to rebuild their empire. They explored new industries, technologies, and markets, embracing change as a catalyst for growth. The entrepreneur's commitment to continuous learning became their greatest asset, enabling them to stay ahead in a rapidly evolving business landscape.

Resilience and resourcefulness played pivotal roles in their resurgence. They formed strategic partnerships, leveraged their network, and sought mentorship from industry leaders. Slowly but steadily, they started to regain lost ground, one calculated step at a time.

The tycoon's unwavering belief in their vision inspired a dedicated team of individuals who shared their passion. Together, they turned adversity into opportunity and transformed setbacks into stepping stones. Their story became a testament to the enduring power of vision and determination.

As they reestablished their presence, the tycoon also prioritized giving back to the community. They launched initiatives to support local businesses, mentor young entrepreneurs, and champion social and environmental causes. Their success was no longer measured solely in financial terms but also in the positive impact they made on the world.

"Resurgence of a Tycoon: A New Chapter After the Fall" is a narrative of triumph over adversity, illustrating that even the most dramatic falls can lead to the most incredible rises. It is a testament to the indomitable spirit of entrepreneurship and the enduring belief that with the right mindset, dedication, and a willingness to adapt, any setback can be a springboard for future success.

Conclusion

"Endless Ascendance: The Ups and Downs of a Contemporary Tycoon" takes us on a captivating journey through the tumultuous world of modern entrepreneurship. In the end, it reminds us that success is often born from resilience, innovation, and an unwavering spirit. As we close this chapter, we're left with the profound understanding that even in the face of adversity, the relentless pursuit of one's dreams can lead to an enduring legacy of triumph.In the pages of "Endless Ascendance: The Ups and Downs of a Contemporary Tycoon," we've witnessed the rollercoaster ride of a remarkable individual, braving storms, overcoming obstacles, and reaching the pinnacle of achievement. It underscores the notion that true tycoons are not just defined by their victories, but by their ability to bounce back from setbacks, reinvent themselves, and keep ascending.

As we reflect on the narrative, it's a testament to the human spirit's indomitable will to conquer the uncharted territories of success. This book serves as a reminder that every twist and turn, every ascent and descent, contributes to the mosaic of a tycoon's life, making it an unforgettable, inspiring, and infinitely captivating tale of ambition and achievement. So, in the end, "Endless Ascendance" encourages us all to reach for the stars, for the only limit to our ascendance is the one we set for ourselves.